ORCA
FOOTPRINTS

Upstream, Downstream

EXPLORING WATERSHED CONNECTIONS

ROWENA RAE

ORCA BOOK PUBLISHERS

Text copyright © Rowena Rae 2021

Published in Canada and the United States
in 2021 by Orca Book Publishers.
orcabook.com

Library and Archives Canada Cataloguing in Publication

Title: Upstream, downstream : exploring
watershed connections / Rowena Rae.
Names: Rae, Rowena, author.
Series: Orca footprints ; 21.
Description: Series statement: Orca footprints ; 21 |
Includes bibliographical references and index.
Identifiers: Canadiana (print) 20210095881 |
Canadiana (ebook) 20210095903 |
ISBN 9781459823921 (hardcover) | ISBN 9781459823938 (PDF) |
ISBN 9781459823945 (EPUB)
Subjects: LCSH: Watersheds—Juvenile literature. |
LCSH: Watershed hydrology—Juvenile literature.
Classification: LCC GB980 .R34 2021 | DDC j551.48—dc23

Library of Congress Control Number: 2020951476

Summary: Part of the nonfiction Orca Footprints
series for middle-grade readers, this book examines
our relationships with watersheds and what we need
to do to protect them for future generations.

Orca Book Publishers is committed to reducing
the consumption of nonrenewable resources in
the making of our books. We make every effort to
use materials that support a sustainable future.

Orca Book Publishers gratefully acknowledges the support
for its publishing programs provided by the following
agencies: the Government of Canada, the Canada Council
for the Arts and the Province of British Columbia through
the BC Arts Council and the Book Publishing Tax Credit.

Front cover photos by susan.k./Getty Images
and Francesco Bergamaschi/Getty Images.
Back cover photos by Christine Phillips/Getty Images,
hadynyah/Getty Images and fenkep/Getty Images.
Design by Teresa Bubela
Layout by Dahlia Yuen
Edited by Kirstie Hudson

Printed and bound in China.

24 23 22 21 • 1 2 3 4

Perito Moreno Glacier in Argentina.
AUMPHOTOGRAPHY/GETTY IMAGES

For my father, who gave me my love of writing.

Contents

Introduction 6

CHAPTER ONE
A WATERY WORLD

Beginning with Basics 8
Nomads by Nature 9
Farming Frenzy 10
Putting Down Roots 11
Stomping on the Earth 16

CHAPTER TWO
THE NUTS AND BOLTS
OF WATERSHEDS

Where the River Runs 18
Where the Lake Stands 19
Wondrous Wetlands 20
Deep Down 20
On the Land 21
Round and Round 22
The Only Constant Is Change 22

CHAPTER THREE
WATERSHEDS IN TROUBLE

Build It Big... 24
Rivers Under Siege.. 26
Demolishing Dams... 27
Water for Rivers.. 28
Water for White Gold..................................... 29
Forests for the Future?................................... 30
Going, Going...Not Quite Gone........................ 33
Paving Over Paradise..................................... 34
Straight as a Ruler.. 35
Lost Streams... 37
Go, Watersheds, Go!...................................... 37

CHAPTER FOUR
WATERSHED WARRIORS!

The Water Walker.. 38
Where Elephants Roam.................................... 39
The Water Man of India................................... 39
The Chocolate Connection............................... 40
Sprouting Roofs.. 41
Connections that Count................................... 42

Resources... 43
Glossary.. 44
Index... 46
Acknowledgments... 48

Introduction

Me at Douglas Creek, near my home.
TRAVIS COMMANDEUR

Ask me for my mailing address, and I'll give you a house number and street name, a city, province and country. Ask me for my *watershed* address, and I'll tell you Douglas Creek, Pacific Ocean. This little creek drains 1,295 acres (524 hectares) of land in my neighborhood and then flows straight into the Pacific Ocean.

I haven't always had such a straightforward watershed address. Years ago I lived in the city of Ottawa, Ontario, and had this address: Rideau River, Ottawa River, St. Lawrence River, Atlantic Ocean.

What's your watershed address? If you shrug your shoulders in answer, you aren't alone! Many people have no idea what their watershed address is, but it's really a good thing to know. Here's why:

First, where does your drinking water come from? From a watershed near you. Where does your home's gray water (washing water) and black water (toilet water) end up? In a watershed near you!

Second, what happens when a forest gets cut down to build houses or when a road gets paved? It changes the land in a watershed. A watershed isn't just the water in an area—it's all

Children enjoying a swim in an Indonesian river.
TI-JA/GETTY IMAGES

the land and everything on the land too. How the land is used can make a big difference to the health of a watershed. And a watershed's health can translate into how much water people and animals have for daily living and how clean that water is.

Third, watersheds the world over are stressed out, thanks mainly to us humans. We've built huge cities, dammed and diverted rivers, cut down vast forests, drained **wetlands** to create farmland and even meddled with the planet's climate. Each of these actions, and lots of others, has an effect on one or more watersheds and all the animals, plants and people that live there.

Once I knew I had a watershed address, I wanted to learn more about what's happening in watersheds near and far. There are amazing things going on, some worrying, some inspiring. Interested in finding out more? Come for a walk with me through the world's watersheds.

CHAPTER ONE

A Watery World

The lower Fraser River near its mouth, seen from an airplane. ROWENA RAE

My Watery World

I grew up in Vancouver, BC, a city with lots of natural beauty—snowcapped mountains, beaches, forests and the Fraser River. This river drains such a large area of land that the entire country of Romania could fit inside its watershed! I've been lucky to see many parts of this long river, from its clear, chattering headwaters 870 miles (1,400 kilometers) inland to its wide, swiftly moving middle to its many-fingered delta and milky-brown exit to the sea. One of my favorite views of the Fraser River is from on high. I'm reminded of the river's grandeur and also of the many ways that people affect it by building and farming nearby, navigating boats and changing the look of the shoreline.

BEGINNING WITH BASICS

What are the two most basic things people need to survive? Water to drink and food to eat. Where do water and food come from? (I mean before they get to your kitchen tap and refrigerator.)

Water comes from lakes, rivers and streams and from *precipitation*—rain, snow and fog. Food also comes from lakes, rivers and streams, as well as from the ocean and the land. Together, water and land make up watersheds.

The "water" part of the word *watershed* is obvious. The "shed" part comes from an Old English word meaning to divide or separate. It refers to a high point of land where a river starts—its *headwaters* or *source*. At this point the hills and mountains form a ridge that guides precipitation in a certain direction as it begins to tumble downhill. All the water falling on one side of the ridge goes one way, and all the water falling on the other side goes the other way. The watershed is all the land on one side of the ridge *plus* all the water in and on that land. Think of the land as a bowl or basin "catching" the falling or melting precipitation, so another term for a watershed is *catchment basin*.

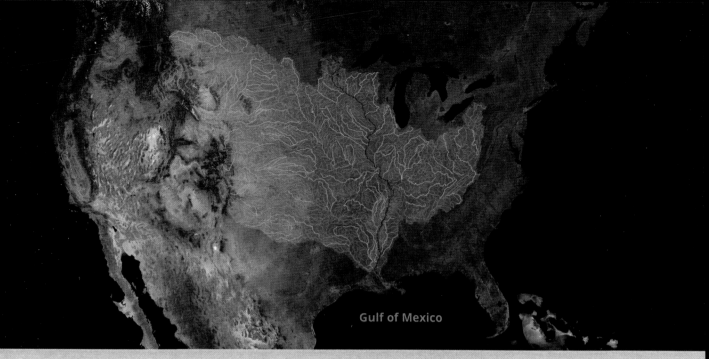

Gulf of Mexico

The Mississippi watershed is the largest catchment basin in North America. This aerial view shows the Mississippi River in dark blue and the smaller rivers and streams that all eventually flow into it. The watershed drains south into the Gulf of Mexico.
HORACE MITCHELL/NASA/GSFC

No matter where you are on the land—whether on a beach at the edge of the sea or in a forest of trees smack in the middle of a continent, you're in a watershed. And no matter where you live—on a farm with miles between you and the neighboring farm or in an apartment on the busiest street of the biggest city, you're in a watershed. Even if you live on an island, as I do, you're in a watershed.

In watersheds, the connections between water and land flow deep (excuse the pun). And these connections are critical for **ecosystems** and all the plants and animals that live in them, including people.

NOMADS BY NATURE

Humans have been around for millions of years. Our species—*Homo sapiens*—began walking on Earth around 300,000 years ago. All early humans lived off the land—literally. They drank from lakes and streams, dewdrops on leaves, and puddles after rainfall. They might have carried a little bit of water with them

Early humans often camped near rivers and lakes. BRIDGEMAN IMAGES

Water taken straight from a stream or lake needs to be filtered, boiled or treated in some other way to make it safe to drink.

STOCKSTUDIOX/GETTY IMAGES

© LOOK AND LEARN/BRIDGEMAN IMAGES

Ripples

One of the earliest ways to lift a large amount of water from a stream or lake was to use a long pole with a bucket on one end and a counterweight on the other end. The pole was mounted like a seesaw. Called a shaduf in Egypt and a denkli in India, this device was in use about 5,000 years ago and in some places is still used today.

in a folded leaf or an animal skin. They followed animal herds, learned which were the best fishing spots and paid attention to the seasons and to which plants produced food when.

The food- and water-gathering activities of early humans affected the local environment where they lived. If they killed an elk calf to eat, that calf wouldn't grow up to have its own calves. If they used fire to cook the meat, there would be fewer branches and sticks to decompose in the forest and some air pollution from the burning wood. If they slipped and slid down an unstable riverbank to get water, some of the soil would fall into the water and smother insect larvae or fish eggs.

These effects were small and in small areas. As human history marched along, people started learning how to get more from the land and water. They got better and better at manipulating—which means using or changing something in a skillful way—their environment to get what they wanted. And the more they manipulated their environment, the bigger and more widespread the effects became.

FARMING FRENZY

People's relationship to land and water changed when farming began about 10,000 years ago in the Middle East and, a bit later, in China and the Americas. It takes land to grow crops, and it takes water to keep seedlings from drying up. The perfect place to farm was on land alongside large rivers that flooded their banks every year. Not only did this land get a surge of water in every flood season, but the water brought sediments—fine particles of sand, soil and clay containing nutrients. As floodwaters drained away, these sediments, often called silt, settled onto the land, making it very *fertile*, or rich in nutrients.

The Nile River in Egypt has a particularly large *delta*. The river branches into many fingers that spill into the Mediterranean Sea. Some of the earliest agriculture in

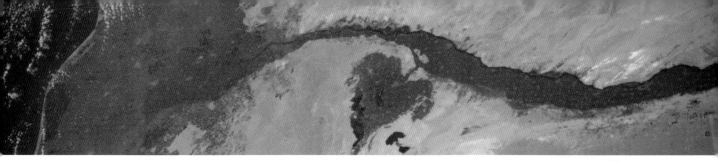
Greenery borders the Nile River. The river delta, at far left, opens into the Mediterranean Sea. JOHNSON SPACE CENTER/NASA

the world started in the Nile River's delta and in nearby Mesopotamia (present-day Iraq and Iran), where two big rivers, the Tigris and the Euphrates, flow into the Persian Gulf.

Relying on floods worked well—at least when the floods came. For many months of the year there weren't any floodwaters. And some years were drier and some were wetter. So after several thousand years of farming by the cycles of nature, people started making the water go where they wanted it to go. This was the beginning of artificial *irrigation*. People dug ditches to direct water to their fields. They blocked rivers with *dams* and *weirs* to send the water in particular directions. They built ponds to keep some water for later use. These efforts helped to control the water flowing onto cultivated land to grow crops.

PUTTING DOWN ROOTS

What did farming give people? Food! That seems obvious, but there's more to it. As agriculture and irrigation got more efficient, food became more abundant. People didn't have to wander over large areas looking for their lunch, so they could settle down and stay in a single spot.

Villages sprang up, and some of them got quite big. Over time, more and more people populated towns and cities that covered large areas of land. And, because humans need water to survive, people developed ingenious ways to tap into (sorry, another pun) nature's liquid gold. Water, that is.

I could write a whole book just about past *civilizations* and how they prospered by changing the land and manipulating waterways for their own purposes. Let me tell you about a few of them.

Ripples
The oldest known wells are on the island of Cyprus in the eastern Mediterranean Sea. They were dug 6.5 feet (2 meters) wide and 26 feet (8 meters) deep to reach water in the ground. These wells were dug at least 10,000 years ago!

The ancient city of Angkor, in today's Cambodia, thrived because its people controlled and stored monsoon rains. After the civilization collapsed, the jungle took over the buildings.
SERGEYCHERNOV/DREAMSTIME.COM

From Black to White

The Sumerian people living on the fertile land between the Tigris and Euphrates Rivers formed the world's first civilization—a complex human society with cultural practices and technologies. The Sumerians lived from approximately 5000 BCE to about 1600 BCE. Their largest settlement, called Uruk, had the distinction of being the world's first city. It had at least 20,000 residents.

The Sumerians built a network of canals, or artificial waterways, to bring fresh water to the people living in Uruk and other smaller towns, to transport goods on barges and to irrigate crops like wheat and barley.

While irrigation canals and dams allowed the Sumerian civilization to grow, they may also have contributed to its downfall. That's because, over time, irrigating the land a lot, especially in hot climates, causes **salinization**. This happens when water **evaporates** and leaves salts behind in the soil. Salinization spells trouble for plants because their roots have a harder time taking up water. The salts build up in the soil and become toxic to many crops.

Salinization is a huge problem today in many parts of the world—especially in Africa, Asia and Australia. In Sumerian times, as the rich, black soil became more crusted with white salts, it most likely led to disaster, with year after year of bad harvests.

Salinization of soil affects croplands in many parts of the world.
ARMASTAS/GETTY IMAGES

Archaeologists study how ancient civilizations used the land and water. SEANSHOT/GETTY IMAGES

The Aqueduct of Valens in Istanbul, Turkey, was built in the late 300s CE. THOMAS WYNESS/DREAMSTIME.COM

Amazing Aqueducts

In Europe, northern Africa and western Asia, the Romans built extraordinary water-moving structures called **aqueducts**—each one a series of pipes, tunnels, canals and bridges—to carry water for long distances. The Romans completed their first aqueduct in 312 BCE and built dozens more during the next 500 or so years. The Romans weren't the first to build aqueducts, but theirs made an especially complex network across the land.

Some Roman aqueducts carried water from more than 50 miles (80 kilometers) away. Starting at a natural source, such as a lake or a spring, an aqueduct went along at a gentle downward angle so the water flowed downhill. Eventually it tumbled into a city **reservoir** (a holding tank or artificial lake). From there the water went through pipes to spout from taps and fountains, to flush away the waste (pee and poop, folks) from public toilets and to fill the famous Roman baths.

The Romans used water for other purposes too. Water irrigated their agricultural fields, turned waterwheels at mills where grains were ground into flour and was jetted into loose soils to make it easier to find gold and other metals.

The Dujiangyan irrigation system on the Minjiang River in China. The river is flowing downstream into the distance. The red dot marks the artificial island. SLEEPINGPANDA/SHUTTERSTOCK.COM

This girl is paddling on a canal in Cambodia.
HADYNYAH/GETTY IMAGES

Crazy for Canals

China has a long history of harnessing rivers for human needs. One of the country's major transport routes, the Grand Canal, is an artificial river linking five large natural rivers. The canal allows boats to carry grain, rice and other products over long distances. The Grand Canal project began in 468 BCE, and over the next 17 centuries (yup, a 1,700-year project) it was lengthened to form a corridor between Beijing in the northeast and Hangzhou in the central east. It's the world's oldest and longest canal (1,115 miles/1,794 kilometers), and it is still well used today.

The ancient Chinese also designed huge irrigation projects. In about 270 BCE, construction began on Dujiangyan, a system to control the Minjiang River, which is a ***tributary*** of (meaning it flows into) the huge Yangtze River. The idea was to lessen annual flooding and deliver water to farmlands. The ingenious part of this project was how the Chinese worked with natural river forces rather than against them.

Instead of building a dam to divert water, the man in charge—Li Bing—had an artificial island built in the middle of the river to split it into two channels. With the help of ***dikes*** (walls built along the channel) and floodgates, the first channel took floodwaters downstream. The second would carry water toward farmland. But there was one problem. A mountain stood in the way of the second channel.

Bing's solution was to tunnel through it. Explosives like gunpowder and dynamite hadn't been invented yet, so Bing's men heated, cooled and then smashed the rocks. After about 10 years the tunnel was complete, and the second river channel began irrigating rice paddies year-round. This ancient irrigation system still waters a vast area of farmland today.

Chop, Chop, Timber!

In Europe, the fall of the Roman Empire marked the beginning of the Middle Ages, or medieval period, which lasted from about 500 to 1500 CE. During this time, people in Europe built hundreds of thousands of waterwheels on streams and rivers. If you've ever stood in the water at the edge of a swiftly flowing stream, you know that water currents can be strong. Waterwheels used that power to grind grain, hammer iron, saw wood, press paper, crush olives—you name it, a tool run on water power may well have done it.

During the Middle Ages, Europeans were also busy cutting down trees. Lots and lots of trees. They used the wood for fuel and construction, and they used the cleared land for crops and animal pastures. This **deforestation** changed local waterflow patterns over the land (more on how this happens in chapter 3). It also set the stage for an invention that changed human existence: the steam engine.

Steaming Up

By the 1600s most of England's trees had been cut down, so people turned to coal as fuel. Coal mining was tied to water in two ways. First, people dug canals so they could transport the coal by boat. Second, as coal mines went deeper and deeper, more **groundwater** seeped into the mines. For a mine near a stream or river, it wasn't such a big deal. A waterwheel could

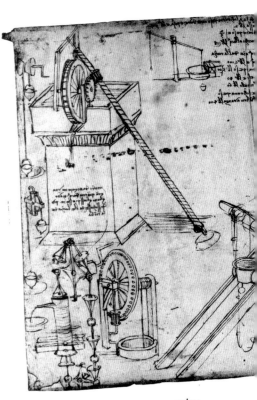

A page of designs for water-moving devices, drawn by Leonardo da Vinci.
©GIANCARLO COSTA/BRIDGEMAN IMAGES

Ripples

Leonardo da Vinci, who lived from 1452 to 1519, designed many gadgets and machines, including water-powered mills, water-lifting devices, locks to get boats through a canal system, and single-span bridges.

A steam engine in 1851.
PHILIP HENRY DELAMOTTE/PURCHASED AS THE
GIFT OF THE RICHARD KING MELLON FOUNDATION/
COURTESY NATIONAL GALLERY OF ART, WASHINGTON

*Car-assembly plants use many
different natural resources.*
RICAGUIAR/GETTY IMAGES

power a pump to get the water out of the mine. But for mines farther from water sources, it was a tiresome process to haul the water out with horses pulling buckets on ropes. People needed a different solution.

Thomas Savery, a military engineer and inventor, built the first steam engine to pump water out of mines in 1698. Other inventors came up with new designs, and by the 1770s James Watt, a Scottish mechanical engineer, had made significant improvements to an earlier steam engine design. The use of Watt's machines took off. Within a few decades, steam engines were not only pumping out mine water but also powering paper, flour and cotton mills and other industries. They went on to power trains, ships and factories.

The use of steam engines started the **Industrial Revolution** and shifted the economy—the way a society makes money—from agriculture to manufacturing.

STOMPING ON THE EARTH

What, you ask, does the Industrial Revolution have to do with watersheds? Everything!

It changed human lifestyles and relationships with land and water, especially as industrialization spread across the planet. People powered tools less and less with water flowing over waterwheels and more and more with engines fueled by coal, oil and other fossil fuels.

The global population exploded and began gobbling up more and more natural resources, including trees, land, metals and water. At the same time, people began dumping all sorts of dangerous things back into nature—things like polluted air, dirty water, chemical pesticides and trash.

I don't mean to suggest that people living in the ancient world didn't make a mark on watersheds. They did, and in many of the same ways we do today. It's just that once the Industrial

Human activities have enormous impacts on water, land and air. DEDMITYAY/SHUTTERSTOCK.COM

Revolution began, the pace of human-created, or **anthropogenic**, changes exploded. Human activity was no longer limited by using animal energy or small waterwheels.

Think about it this way. When you step in mud, your foot changes the way the mud looks. It makes a footprint. When human activities "step" in watersheds—that is, use water and land resources—we change them. We make an environmental or *ecological footprint*.

During the past 250 years—*only* 250 years—our ecological footprint has gotten pretty big. According to the Global Footprint Network, humans currently use the ecological resources of one and three-quarter Earths. Gulp! This cannot keep going—it isn't sustainable. We're not so much stepping in watersheds as stomping all over them.

The thing is, the water and the land remain connected, but human actions are injuring them and thereby damaging their connections. Think about a hockey or basketball team. A player with a sore ankle or sprained finger can still play the game but not very well. As a result the whole team suffers. The same thing happens in watersheds. If the individual waterways and pieces of the landscape are injured, they don't work very well, and the whole watershed is worse off.

To better understand *how* we're affecting watersheds, we first need to know the different parts of the water and land in a watershed.

Ripples
Lots of things we take for granted today were invented during the Industrial Revolution—light bulbs, telephones, electric motors, internal-combustion engines and cars.

The Nuts and Bolts of Watersheds

Hanging Glacier in Chile sends water cascading into the Rio (River) Ventisqueros watershed.
CHRISTINE PHILLIPS/GETTY IMAGES

WHERE THE RIVER RUNS

At their headwaters in mountains and on hilltops, rivers start as tiny trickles from falling rain or melting snow and ice. Some rivers start from melting **glaciers**. As you probably already know, glaciers are disappearing at a speedy pace as climate change warms up the regions where these "rivers of ice" tend to be. Trickles of meltwater and rain form little rivulets that gather in creeks. A few creeks merge into a stream, and a few streams join to become a river. Each bit of flowing water is a tributary of the bigger one it joins.

Because of gravity—the force attracting things on Earth to the center of the planet—water always flows downhill. On steep mountainsides, therefore, rivulets and creeks tumble downhill in a babbling frenzy. As the land becomes less steep, the creeks and streams babble less but continue to flow steadily downward.

When the water reaches flatter land, the volume, or amount, of water is so large that the river now has a lot of energy. The flowing water **erodes**, or chips away at, the riverbanks and winds back and forth across the land to use up some of its energy. This is called meandering. The wide bends in large rivers are **meanders**.

Eventually a large river spreads out in a delta that looks like the end of a fraying ribbon, with each thread spilling its water into the sea. Now that it's lost some of its energy, the river water deposits the sediments carried from inland, and they build up as low-lying islands. The islands in deltas contain fertile land, and for this reason, river deltas all over the world have been made into farmlands.

The river water mixes with tidal ocean water, creating a rich environment called an **estuary**. Estuaries are productive nurseries for fish, and they attract lots of birds and other wildlife. An estuary is at a river's **outflow** or **mouth**—the place where the river ends.

The land on either side of the river, along its entire length, from headwaters to mouth, is called the **riparian zone**. Plants growing in this fertile, moist land are as important to a river as the water itself. The riparian zone soaks up and stores water, keeps soil in place, shades the water and provides habitat for dozens of creatures.

WHERE THE LAKE STANDS

When depressions or dips in the land fill with water, they become lakes. Many lakes are small, better described as ponds. Other lakes, like the North American Great Lakes, are too big to see across from one shore to the other. For example, the largest of these lakes, Lake Superior, is 350 miles (563 kilometers) long and 160 miles (257 kilometers) wide.

Lakes are sometimes called *standing water* because the water in them doesn't flow as fast as rivers do. But lakes don't just collect water and never let it go again. Water flows into most lakes from rivers and streams, gets mixed around by the wind and eventually flows out by a different river or stream, called the lake's outflow. The pace is simply slower than in a river. In some lakes, water passes through in a few days or weeks. Lake St. Clair, which lies between Lake Huron and Lake Erie, keeps its water for about seven days. In others, water stays for many decades or even centuries before flowing back out. It takes 173 years for water to pass through Lake Superior.

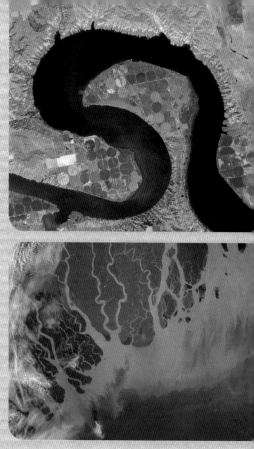

(Top) A meander in the Missouri River, South Dakota. (Bottom) The Ganges River Delta in Bangladesh and India.
(TOP) NASA/GSFC/METI/ERSDAC/JAROS AND U.S./ JAPAN ASTER SCIENCE TEAM / (BOTTOM) JOHNSON SPACE CENTER/NASA

Ripples
Some deltas, like the Mississippi River Delta (below), look like the foot of a bird when viewed from the sky. The river deposits its load of sediments faster than ocean waves and the tide can spread them out. Over time this forms a bird-foot delta.

JOHNSON SPACE CENTER/NASA

Birds such as these cranes feed in wetlands.
BIGWORLD/GETTY IMAGES

WONDROUS WETLANDS

You had probably heard of rivers and lakes before reading this book, but what about marshes, bogs, fens and swamps? These are all examples of wetlands. And they're exactly what the word *wetland* suggests—wet patches of land. That may not sound exciting, but wetlands are places with lots of nutrients and a huge variety of plants, insects, amphibians, fish, birds and other animals. With so much plant and animal life, wetlands are some of the most productive ecosystems in the world. That is, they produce or make a home for a great many living things. Wetlands also have important jobs. They filter and clean water by stripping out pollutants. In your body, this job is done by your kidneys. That's why you might hear wetlands being called nature's kidneys. Wetlands also keep floodwaters under control by collecting and holding water for a while, a bit like your bladder. And, keeping the body comparison going, they transform nutrients, like your digestive system does!

DEEP DOWN

These three main types of waterbody—rivers, lakes and wetlands—are called surface waters, because they are on top of the land. There's also underground water, or groundwater. When water seeps into the ground (and doesn't get sucked up by a plant's roots), it becomes groundwater. Water keeps moving downward in the ground until it gets to a zone where all the cracks and pores in the rocks are filled, or *saturated*, with water. The top of the saturated zone is the *water table*, and all the water in the saturated zone is an *aquifer*. Water wells are drilled through the ground into an aquifer so that people can pull or pump water up to the surface.

One of the largest aquifers in the world is the Ogallala Aquifer beneath the Great Plains of the United States. It could cover the entire country (including Alaska and Hawaii) in 1.5 feet (just under half a meter) of water. Groundwater doesn't just hang out underground. It moves around. Some seeps into the sea, and some refreshes wetlands, streams and lakes from below.

ON THE LAND

The land in a watershed includes the mountains that I've already talked about and also forests, grasslands, scrublands and deserts. Each of these is a type of *land cover*, and each one can be further divided into specific types. For example, forests can be woodlands of mainly *deciduous* trees or temperate rainforests in cool climates or jungle rainforests in warm climates.

Land cover is what nature has placed on the land. When humans came along, they started using the land for specific purposes. *Land use* is what people do on or with land, such as growing crops, grazing animals, building towns and cities, constructing roads and pipelines, harvesting trees, mining, drilling and other industrial activities.

Why should we know such specific things about land cover and land use in a watershed? Because they all play a part in a water droplet's journey through that watershed. This journey is tied to the *water cycle*.

The banks of the Kvirila River in Georgia have both natural land cover and human land uses.
ZDENEK ADAMEC/DREAMSTIME.COM

A water-cycle diagram shows where and how water moves on Earth.
ADAPTED FROM VECTORMINE/SHUTTERSTOCK.COM

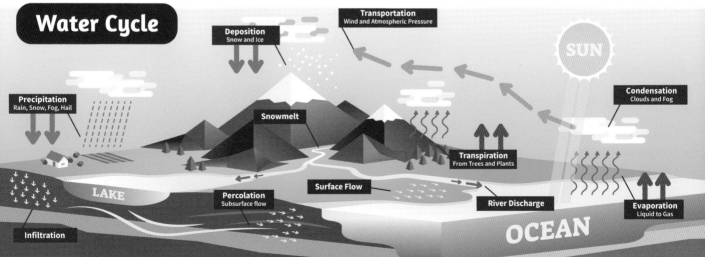

Water Cycle

Precipitation
Rain, Snow, Fog, Hail

Deposition
Snow and Ice

Transportation
Wind and Atmospheric Pressure

SUN

Condensation
Clouds and Fog

Snowmelt

Transpiration
From Trees and Plants

LAKE

Percolation
Subsurface flow

Surface Flow

River Discharge

Evaporation
Liquid to Gas

Infiltration

OCEAN

Over time the Colorado River has cut a path to create Marble Canyon in Arizona.
BENEDEK/GETTY IMAGES

ROUND AND ROUND

Nature loves cycles—something going from one phase to another and another and yet another and then back to the beginning to go around again. The water cycle, also called the **hydrologic cycle**, takes a water droplet around the world through different phases—liquid, gas and solid. Liquid water evaporates from oceans and lakes and gets carried as a gas through the atmosphere. Later it turns back into a liquid to fall as rain or into a solid to fall as snow or hail.

When this precipitation falls on land, it enters a watershed. Whatever is on the land affects a water droplet's journey through the water cycle. Depending on where it falls, the droplet could stay frozen as snow for a short while, or it could get compacted into a glacier and stay frozen for a long time. Or it could flow into a river, lake or wetland. There the droplet could be drunk by an animal. It could evaporate straight back into the atmosphere. It could soak into the ground and be drawn up by the roots of a plant and later released from the plant's leaves in the process of **transpiration**. The droplet could descend into an aquifer. Or it could eventually flow all the way out to the ocean.

If precipitation falls on a farm, it could mix first with some fertilizer before running off into a nearby stream. If it falls in an urban area, it could cascade along a paved road, collecting pollutants, before tumbling into a storm sewer and from there draining into the ocean. If it falls on a hillside cleared of its trees, it could push and pull the unstable soil downhill into a babbling creek.

Ripples
If all the glaciers on Earth were to melt, sea level would be about 230 feet (70 meters) higher than it is today.

THE ONLY CONSTANT IS CHANGE

Watersheds are happening places. Nothing stays still—things are always changing. For example, the seasons can bring dramatic changes. In the Fraser River watershed in British Columbia, snowmelt from the mountains feeds streams and the river with gushing water in an event called the spring **freshet**.

In the Amazon River watershed in South America, heavy rainfall drenches the land during monsoon season. At these times, so much rain falls that rivers can swell in the blink of an eye and spill over their banks to submerge parts of the adjacent land. That flooded land is the river's *floodplain*.

During dry seasons, the amount of water in a river can decline and sometimes be so low that sections of the riverbed become dry. This can happen naturally, but as you'll read in the next chapter, people play a significant role in drying up the world's watery places.

Changes in watersheds happen on geologic scales too. Over millions of years, flowing streams and rivers cut into the rocks and shape the land. For example, the Colorado River has been flowing over layers of *sedimentary* rock for about five million years. The river gradually carved away the rocks in northern Arizona to form the deep (6,000 feet/1,830 meters at its deepest) and wide (18 miles/29 kilometers at its widest) Grand Canyon. Wow!

Changes to watersheds also happen with massive natural disturbances such as earthquakes and volcanoes. These events can clog a riverbed with debris or even disrupt a river's flow, sending it off in a different direction. Large volcanic eruptions can affect rainfall patterns. This means that river volume and flow can change in countries far away from the eruption.

Seasonal cycles, geological time and natural disturbances are part of any watershed's life story. But they aren't the only kind of changes watersheds experience. Since the dawn of humankind (that's us and our ancestors!), watersheds have been subjected to human, or anthropogenic, disturbances. That's basically all those land uses I was talking about earlier.

Humans around the world have changed watersheds for thousands of years. But what about our modern civilization? How are people today changing the world's watersheds? And are the changes causing problems?

Let's find out.

The ice on Lake Vanda is as thick as the ice auger I'm holding is high. That is, the ice is about 10 feet (3 meters) thick!
ROB SMITH

My Watery World

As a university student, I spent two weeks in the McMurdo Dry Valleys region of Antarctica. With other biologists, I flew by helicopter to Lake Vanda, a permanently ice-covered lake with no outflow to the sea. We camped and measured light, temperature and algae in the water below the ice. The lake's watershed contains just rocks, sand, glaciers, an inflowing creek, a few algae and lichens. Without animals or plants in its watershed, Lake Vanda's water is clear and pure. Careless human visitors could easily pollute it. My fellow biologists and I had to be super careful with everything we did and used. Nothing could spill in the watershed. Everything we took in with us had to come back out. And I mean *everything*. Yup, that included our urine (collected in metal drums) and feces (collected in plastic buckets)! When we packed up to leave, our scientific gear, tents, backpacks and waste containers all jostled together in the mesh sling carried beneath the helicopter.

CHAPTER THREE

Watersheds in Trouble

BUILD IT BIG

What do you get when you take 21 yellow school buses (the standard ones that seat about 60 passengers), tip them on end and stack them up nose to tail? The height of Hoover Dam (726 feet/221 meters).

Hoover Dam is a massive, curved concrete structure on the Colorado River, at the state line between Nevada and Arizona. It's an impressive structure. When construction finished in 1936, it was the world's tallest dam. It backs up and holds river water in a reservoir (an artificial lake) called Lake Mead. This water irrigates thousands of acres of farmland in California and Arizona. The dam also has an adjacent power plant where the force of the Colorado River gets turned into electricity as the water flows through turbines, which are a bit like waterwheels with blades. Millions of people in the southwestern states get their electricity from Hoover Dam.

Hoover Dam is no longer the world's tallest. Today it doesn't even rank in the world's top 20! In less than a century, people have built thousands of tall dams on rivers. An organization called International Rivers estimates that the world has more than 57,000 large dams—dams higher than 50 feet (15 meters).

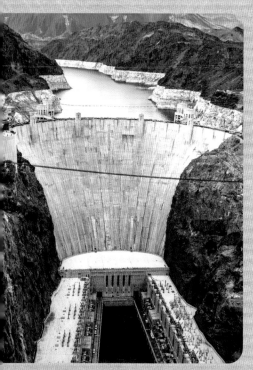

Hoover Dam took five years to build and enough concrete to pave a road 16 feet (5 meters) wide between San Francisco and New York City.
EYFOTO/GETTY IMAGES

High in an alpine area of Austria, a tall dam holds back the water in Mooserboden Reservoir.
TYUKODI LSZL / EYEEM/GETTY IMAGES

In Washington State, Elwha River water rushes through open floodgates at the Glines Canyon Dam in 2013, the year before the dam was demolished.
U.S. NATIONAL PARK SERVICE

Add those to the hundreds of thousands of smaller dams and weirs that block, divert or interrupt rivers, and the big numbers can make your head swim.

People need to drink water, and they need to eat food, which is grown on irrigated fields and pastures. And in our modern society we need power to run our appliances and tools. Dams help provide the water for these things, and they have other benefits. They can help reduce flooding along riverbanks and make boat transport safer. All good things, right?

Well, yes and no. Everything has benefits and costs, and large dams have rather a lot of costs. I'm not talking about money—though, of course, building a large dam is an expensive project. I'm talking about costs to the environment and to local people.

A salmon jumps into a pool of water at a fish ladder, the only way for the salmon to get above the dam that blocks its migration upstream. MANON RINGUETTE/DREAMSTIME.COM

RIVERS UNDER SIEGE

Here's a list of environmental costs from dams.

- They block animals, especially fish, from swimming up- or downstream. This is a particularly big problem for salmon and other species that use both freshwater and ocean habitats during their lives.
- They flood the land upstream from the dam to create a reservoir. With large dams, whole valleys become covered with water—the forests, the meadows, the wetlands. That's a lot of fertile land destroyed, not to mention the habitats and the plants and animals living there. And the submerged vegetation—trees, bushes, grasses—releases greenhouse gases as it rots, or decomposes, at the bottom of the reservoir. Reservoir emissions are about 1.5 percent of the world's greenhouse gas emissions from anthropogenic sources.
- They alter the riverbed downstream. Dam operators can change the volume and timing of water flowing over a dam, which changes the river below the dam. Rivers rely on floods to build their channels and enrich their floodplains and riparian zones with wood, sediments and nutrients. Dams hold these back. The losers are the downstream river channel, the floodplain and all the organisms living in and near the river.
- They dramatically change life for many people. Those living on land destined to become a reservoir are displaced—literally flooded off the land—when a dam becomes operational. A lot of people around the world—as many as 40 to 80 million—have experienced this fate. The displaced are often Indigenous Peoples and farmers with small farms. Being forcefully removed from one's home is a terrible experience that has repercussions for generations, especially for Indigenous Peoples who are removed from traditional territories. They can no longer access family and community hunting and fishing grounds. Cultural sites become

On the 2020 Day of Action for Rivers, these two girls protest a proposed dam in Myanmar. SAW MORT

inaccessible or destroyed. Farmers no longer have a source of livelihood. People who have been removed from their homes live in increased poverty and experience mental and emotional trauma.

DEMOLISHING DAMS

Are the environmental and social costs of dams worth it to have the irrigated farmlands, drinking water and electricity? Food and water are basic human needs, and electricity has become a basic human need in our modern society. What to do? It's complicated, and I don't have the answer (sorry!). The large power-generating dams already built are likely here to stay, but there are some examples of dams being removed to let rivers run free again.

Two large dams were recently demolished on the Elwha River in Washington State. They had been built in the early 1900s to power industries in the growing town of Port Angeles. The town later connected to a different power grid (coming from the Columbia River), and the Lower Elwha Klallam Tribe requested that the dams be removed. When the dams were built, salmon could no longer swim up much of the river during their annual spawning runs. This loss of valuable salmon affected the Lower Elwha Klallam Tribe's food system and changed their lives and relationship with the land for many generations.

The removal took decades of negotiations, but finally both dams came down. Salmon once again swim upstream to spawn, and sediments and wood get carried downstream to replenish the river's estuary. Dam-removal projects are immense tasks and won't be possible in many places, but sometimes they may be the right thing to do.

By now you've got the idea that watersheds are complex places. Their web of connections extends beyond the natural world to affect social and political worlds too.

This old dam on Britannia Creek in British Columbia was dismantled.
COURTESY MARK ANGELO

The crater of Mount St. Helens presides over the new stream channels running down to the plains below.
ROWENA RAE

My Watery World

When Mount St. Helens in Washington State erupted on May 18, 1980, I was asleep in bed in Vancouver, BC. Thirty-four years later, I visited the mountain. Many things struck me, especially the raw beauty of the mountain and how it is recreating its watershed. All down the sides of the plain where the lava flowed, meltwater has cut new stream channels. Grasses and shrubs have sprouted. I saw a herd of elk grazing in the distance. Even after catastrophic disturbances, nature can heal and refashion watersheds.

WATER FOR RIVERS

Water diversion—sending water from one place to another—began with the earliest human civilizations. Diversion can be as small as piping a little bit of creek water onto a nearby veggie patch or as big as the Snowy Mountains Scheme in Australia. This monster of a project took 25 years to build, which isn't surprising when you hear that more than 100,000 people were involved in constructing 16 major dams, 7 power-generation stations, 50 miles (80 kilometers) of aqueducts and 90 miles (145 kilometers) of tunnels through mountains. Sounds like the sort of project Li Bing would have undertaken had he lived a millennium and a half later!

Before the project began, the Snowy River flowed southeast and eventually drained into the Tasman Sea. After the project was completed in 1974, an astounding 99 percent of the river's water was diverted! The project sent the water through the newly built tunnels to flow in a totally different direction—west into the Murray and Murrumbidgee Rivers that drain into the Great Australian Bight (the large open bay on the south side of the Australian continent). The diverted water irrigates farmlands, and the hydroelectricity powers hundreds of thousands of homes.

The Snowy River was left with barely any water flow. And other changes happened too. More sediments got stuck in the river channel because water flows weren't strong enough to flush them downstream. Shallow sections of the river warmed up, harming fish, frogs and other organisms. Connections were lost between the river and nearby wetlands that depended on floodwaters to recharge them. These and more watershed changes meant less habitat and less food for the iconic Australian platypus, waterbirds and a host of other organisms. Since the early 2000s, the Snowy River has been receiving more of its natural water flow in an effort to restore some of these habitats.

WATER FOR WHITE GOLD

Last century a water-diversion disaster dramatically shrank the Aral Sea, the world's fourth-largest lake, which straddles the border between Kazakhstan and Uzbekistan. This lake has an internal watershed, meaning it's not connected to the ocean. Water leaves only by seeping into the ground and by evaporating. Over thousands of years, water evaporates from this kind of lake and leaves behind salts, so the water becomes saline.

In the early 1900s, the Aral Sea had about 10 parts of salt in every 1,000 parts of water. Think of a large quilt made up of 1,000 squares. In the Aral Sea, 10 of those squares were salt. In the ocean, 35 squares are salt.

In about 1960, the government of the former Soviet Union began diverting the Aral Sea's two inflowing rivers, the Syr Darya and the Amu Darya. The water went to irrigate the surrounding desert, mainly to grow cotton—"white gold"—for export. Canals were built in the 1930s, and within three decades the lake began to shrink. And it kept shrinking and shrinking until it was just 10 percent of its former size.

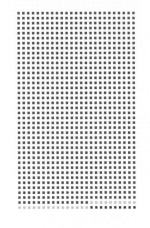

This "water quilt" has 1,000 squares. The Aral Sea contains 990 squares of water (blue and yellow) and 10 squares of salt (red). The ocean has 965 water (blue) and 35 salt (yellow and red). In fresh water, less than one half of one square is salt and the rest of the squares are water.

In August 2018 the Aral Sea consisted of a few greenish-blue lakes. The white areas are crusted salt. The yellow line shows the approximate shoreline in 1960, and the red dot is on the town of Mo'ynoq, Uzbekistan.
NASA EARTH OBSERVATORY

The Aral Sea is littered with the rusting hulks of abandoned boats. This boy climbed onto one of them near Mo'ynoq, Uzbekistan. MIGUEL BS/SHUTTERSTOCK.COM

Two men fish in one of the small lakes left after the Aral Sea retreated.

The saltiness of the water increased to more than 100 parts per thousand in some bays (100 of the squares on the water quilt). Most of the fish died, and the fishing industry collapsed. The dry lake bed sent dust storms of salt and agricultural pesticides through the air. Thousands of people became ill with cancers, lung diseases and other ailments. In the early 2000s, a restoration project began on the North Aral Sea in today's Kazakhstan. Thanks to that, the lake is getting larger and less salty. Enough fish live there now to support a fishing industry. The South Aral Sea, in today's Uzbekistan, hasn't fared so well. But work is underway to plant shrubby trees on the dry lake bed. Called saxaul trees, they tolerate dry, salty soil, and their roots will stop the wind from lifting and blowing the contaminated soil.

FORESTS FOR THE FUTURE?

Speaking of trees, our planet has a lot of them! Forests cover about one-third of Earth's land. The trees in these forests do so many things it's almost dizzying to think about. They provide shelter and food for all sorts of organisms, from stick insects to woodland caribou, from monkey frogs to humans. They produce oxygen—the gas we need to breathe. They use carbon dioxide—that greenhouse gas we need to reduce in our atmosphere. They play a starring role in the water cycle by pumping water from their roots to their leaves and releasing it into the air. Wow! But wait—trees do even more.

They absorb air pollutants through their leaves. They enrich the soil by dropping their leaves, flowers and fruits to decompose on the forest floor. They stop rain from running straight over the ground and washing away the soil. They keep the forest floor cool.

Trees do these things—called *ecosystem services*—in watersheds all over the world. But trees can't perform these services if they're not growing in the ground. And because of deforestation, more and more trees aren't.

This river in England has not only lost its streamside vegetation, but it also has cows trampling its banks and the river channel.

Forest harvesting changes the look of a landscape, and it alters how water soaks into and runs over the land.
XALANX/DREAMSTIME.COM

Deforestation—literally cutting down forests—threatens watersheds and everything within them (us included) the world over. A lot of forests are cleared for farming, animal grazing, mining, drilling or laying pipelines. The ongoing growth and sprawl of cities contributes too. Wildfires claim forests as well.

Trees are also logged to make building materials, paper and other products. In many countries, logging practices today are more sustainable than they were decades ago. But some logging happens illegally and without much care for impacts on the watershed.

Whether legal or illegal, logging operations need roads to get equipment in and logs back out. These dirt roads get packed down, so during a heavy rainfall, water rushes along the road instead of soaking into the ground. The rushing water erodes the soil, which is swept into streams and fills up the spaces in the gravel on the streambed. By blocking sunlight and oxygen, the soil kills the insect larvae and fish eggs, which means fewer fish, which means less food for the birds, which—you get the picture. It's all about connections.

A community group plants trees and bushes along a stream.
ALYSON SKINNER

Ripples
Since 1900 about one-third of the world's wetlands have been lost.

It's hard to figure out exactly how much deforestation happens worldwide each year. One source uses satellite images to calculate how much tree cover disappears, whether from logging or wildfires. It says about 29 million hectares (72 million acres) disappear in one year. This boils down to the amount of forest to cover 350 ice-hockey rinks being lost every minute. *Every minute!*

Other sources say much less forest is lost—only as much in one minute as would cover 40 ice-hockey rinks. Even so, we're talking about a lot of trees. Part of the difficulty in calculating *de*forestation involves *re*forestation—trees growing back. Some forests don't have a chance to grow back—those cut down to expand cities, create farmlands or dig mines. But other forests do. After a wildfire, nature can recover and grow new trees. After logging, foresters in some countries replant the land with young trees.

Like water, trees are a renewable resource. Plant a seed and you can grow a tree. But it's not quite as easy as planting a whole bunch of seeds and regaining a lost forest. It takes time to establish the web of connections between the trees in a forest and the soil, waterways and air.

Sometimes the best way to appreciate a tree's majesty is to stand at its base and look way, way up! STOCKSTUDIOX/GETTY IMAGES

What do you see in this photo of Houston, TX? A jungle of roads and buildings? How about the stream that looks like it's choked with silt? BRYAN ROSCHETZKY/DREAMSTIME.COM

GOING, GOING...NOT QUITE GONE

An international agreement called the Ramsar Convention has many governments working together to protect wetlands worldwide. They're on a mission, since wetlands are disappearing three times faster than forests. Many wetlands are already long gone—drained and transformed for other uses—but fortunately some still exist. More and more people are realizing the importance of wetlands, not just for animals but also for people.

More than 2,300 wetlands have become Ramsar Wetlands of International Importance, and together they cover an area

Ripples
The United States has more than 4 million miles (6.5 million kilometers) of roads—the longest road network in the world! All these roads change the pattern of water flowing over the land and soaking into the ground.

33

In 30 years the city of Shanghai grew from about 12 million people to roughly 24 million. With population comes urbanization. These images show Shanghai and the surrounding area in the 1980s (top) and the 2010s (bottom).
(TOP & BOTTOM) JOSHUA STEVENS AND JESSE ALLEN/ NASA EARTH OBSERVATORY AND U.S. GEOLOGICAL SURVEY

Grates on the road often lead into storm drains that go directly out to lakes, rivers or the sea. Don't dump anything down them!
FENKEP/GETTY IMAGES

larger than Mexico. Some of them are small, like South Korea's Odaesan National Park Wetlands, which is a group of three fens covering an area the size of just 12.5 ice-hockey rinks. The park is home to several vulnerable species, including the long-tailed goral (a type of wild goat). Other wetlands are immense, like Ngiri-Tumba-Maindombe in the Democratic Republic of Congo. This site covers the same area as Lake Huron, or about 38 million ice-hockey rinks! Part of the Congo River flows through the site, so vegetation in the river's floodplain protects towns from flooding during the rainy season.

Elsewhere, people are recognizing the value of protecting wetlands because of the ecosystem services they perform. New York City operates the largest city water supply in the United States. Most of the city's drinking water comes straight from reservoirs, no filtration needed. No easy feat for a city of 8.5 million people. Can you guess the secret to their success? Yup, wetlands. The city carefully protects the wetlands around its reservoirs. Buying and protecting land costs a lot of money, but not nearly as much as it would cost to build several water-treatment plants. After all, wetlands are nature's water-treatment plants, so if we keep them healthy, they'll do the work for us!

PAVING OVER PARADISE

As cities grow, they spread over more and more land. And inevitably they change how water moves across and into that land. That's because of all the hard surfaces, such as roofs, driveways, roads and parking lots. These surfaces are *impervious*—they prevent water from seeping into the ground. Instead water runs off elsewhere, often into storm drains. On the way to a storm drain, rainwater collects pesticides, fertilizers, oils and whatever else has settled on the street. Storm drains sometimes go to water-treatment facilities, but more often they empty straight into a lake, river or ocean.

In its final stretch, the Los Angeles River in California flows straight—literally—to the ocean. STEVE PROEHL/GETTY IMAGES

STRAIGHT AS A RULER

Many cities have a confined river. What do I mean by that? It means dikes, walls and embankments are built along a river channel to control where it flows. Usually rivers get this treatment because they're prone to flooding. When they are allowed to flow naturally, rivers meander. But if you build structures to force them into a straight channel, you better get out your rubber boots!

When a river loses its meanders, and the wetlands in its floodplain get paved over, the river loses its ability to deal with lots of water. When snowmelt or heavy rains swell the river, the sudden rush of water has nowhere to go but over the concrete embankments. The river no longer has a riparian zone or floodplain wetlands to absorb the water and release it slowly. Instead the surrounding streets, buildings and land get flooded.

Flooding rivers cause millions of dollars in damage every year in communities all over the world, not to mention people losing their homes, their possessions, their livelihoods and sometimes, sadly, their lives. For example, in August and September 2019, heavy monsoon rains fell on the Indian states of Bihar and

Uttar Pradesh, causing the Ganges River to overflow. Car and train traffic stopped, and people used boats and rafts to navigate the roads. Thousands of people were evacuated, and some had to be rescued from their homes. Sewage and garbage got mixed in with the floodwaters. More than 100 people lost their lives.

Similar flooding has happened in recent years in dozens of other parts of the world too. The Ross River burst over its banks in Townsville, Australia, as did the Juba and Shabelle Rivers in Somalia, the Saint John River in New Brunswick, Canada, and the Ciliwung River in Jakarta, Indonesia. In each location, the impacts differed a little—some had more mudslides, some had more people displaced, some had an uptick in mosquito-borne diseases. But in all of these events, a surge of water exceeded the river's ability to deal with the extra flow.

These boys wade home from school through streets that flooded after heavy rains in the city of Guwahati, India. TALUKDAR DAVID/SHUTTERSTOCK.COM

This section of Cheonggyecheon Stream in Seoul, South Korea, has been unburied and now flows open to the daylight. The stream attracts birds, insects and amphibians. The neighborhoods near the stream have cooler and less-polluted air thanks to the flowing water, streamside vegetation, brisker breezes and reduced car traffic. MLENNY/GETTY IMAGES

LOST STREAMS

While many cities turned streams into straight channels, others, like Vancouver in British Columbia, Yonkers in New York and Seoul in South Korea, simply buried them! They forced the water to flow through large pipes and poured concrete over top. These buried streams were left to flow unseen. After a few generations, they often became forgotten too. Rewilding a stream or *daylighting*—literally uncovering the stream to open it up to daylight—is now happening around the world, including in Vancouver, Yonkers and Seoul. The positive results include better stormwater control, improved water quality, habitats for animals to return to and places for citizens to connect with nature.

Ripples
Megacities are cities with more than 10 million inhabitants. In 2018 the world had 33 megacities making a mega-impact on their watersheds.

GO, WATERSHEDS, GO!

How well a watershed functions comes down to how healthy each part of the watershed is and how well each part connects with the others. As with a hockey or basketball team, healthy players play the game well. Injured players don't play so well.

Fortunately many people are working hard to keep watersheds connected or to help reconnect broken ones. In the next chapter, I'll introduce you to a few of these watershed warriors.

Watershed Warriors!

THE WATER WALKER

Josephine Mandamin's mission in life was to treat water with dignity and respect and to lead by example. In 2003 this Elder from Wiikwemkoong First Nation in northern Ontario went for a walk. Not just any walk. She walked all the way around Lake Superior, about 2,700 miles (4,300 kilometers). In later years Josephine walked around the other North American Great Lakes, too, and along the St. Lawrence River and other waterways in the world. In her lifetime Josephine walked many thousands of miles over many months, always carrying a copper pail of water. Her message was the same each time: water must be protected.

When Josephine Mandamin died in 2019, Autumn Peltier took over her great-aunt's work. Autumn began her own journey to protect water when she was just eight years old, after visiting an Indigenous community where the water was too polluted to drink. That seemed wrong to her. She started speaking out, and five years later, as a 13-year-old, Autumn spoke to a gathering of world leaders at the United Nations. Her message to them? "Warrior up!" she said. "Our water deserves to be treated as human with human rights."

Josephine Mandamin carries a copper pail of water during a "water walk."
AYŞE GÜRSÖZ

Elephants and many other animals in Africa depend on Okavango River and its delta. SUNGMOON HAN / EYEEM/GETTY IMAGES

WHERE ELEPHANTS ROAM

In the African country of Angola, Adjany Costa grew up knowing only one part of nature—the beach. She and her family couldn't visit other natural places because civil war made it too unsafe. When the war finally ended, Adjany went to the Okavango River for the first time. She traveled across the border to Botswana to see the Okavango Delta, which is part of an internal watershed, so it doesn't flow to the sea. Instead the waters eventually sink into the sand. Before they do, they create a rich wetland known as a *biodiversity hotspot*—it's home to an exceptionally wide array of species, including elephants, impalas, hippos, egrets and cranes. Adjany was in awe of the vast wilderness.

She also visited the river's headwaters in the highlands of Angola and realized how the entire Okavango Delta relies on the water coming from two rivers in her country. She started working with the Luchaze people living in the Angolan highlands to protect the watershed. But because they had been displaced from their lands during the war, the Luchaze's connection with the land had been disrupted. Adjany works with Elders in the communities to document their stories about the forests and rivers and create books for the younger generation to help them reconnect.

THE WATER MAN OF INDIA

As a young man, Rajendra Singh trained as a medic. Then he went to small villages in the Indian state of Rajasthan to set up health clinics. But the villagers told him they needed something

Rajendra Singh explains to farmers how they can harvest water for their cattle.
SIDDHARTHA KUMAR/DPA/AGEFOTOSTOCK

My Watery World

My family used to live in a small town called Summerland in a desertlike part of British Columbia. One summer we had a drought—a severe water shortage—and the local creek that supplied the town's water nearly went dry. It had such low flow that fish were dying. Every home received a notice with strict instructions about water use. To do our part, we stopped showering every day. We washed dishes in a plastic tub and poured the gray water on vegetable beds. We also let the grass go brown outside our home, and we've done this ever since. The grass doesn't die—it just waits for the fall rains. Then it turns as green as...well, as green as grass!

else much more than they needed healthcare. They needed water. Their wells were dry and their farmlands parched. Sand and dust blew about the villages. Rajendra listened and thought. He learned about traditional methods of gathering and storing rainwater and decided to put them back into use.

Together, Rajendra and the villagers built earthen dams called johads. These crescent-shaped structures are made of packed mud and rocks. When monsoon rains come, they hold back some of the water. By trapping water and pooling it, the johads can be used to prevent flooding, and they also give water a chance to seep into the ground. Over time Rajendra's johads began to refill local aquifers and restore water flow to some rivers.

His successes got noticed, and many more villages asked him to help them too. For more than 30 years, Rajendra has been working all over India, helping to build thousands of johads in more than 500 villages.

In 2015 Rajendra received the Stockholm Water Prize, the world's top award for people who are working to conserve and protect water and watersheds.

THE CHOCOLATE CONNECTION

On Christmas Day 2016, Typhoon Nock-Ten hammered the Philippines. In the area where Louise Mabulo lives, the storm flattened most of the farmland. The teenage chef started helping out by finding seeds and growing seedlings so the farmers could replant their fields. But she also wondered what else could be done to lessen the devastation to farmers from future typhoons.

Louise noticed that cacao trees—which give us chocolate—had stayed standing through and after the typhoon. And as a chef, she knew cacao is a valuable product that can bring farmers a good income. So she started the Cacao Project to provide seedlings to farmers. Cacao trees take a few years to start producing

Louise Mabulo talks about cacao trees and their fruit—cacao pods—with schoolchildren in the Philippines.
ZALRIAN SAYAT AND KYLE MOLINA

a steady crop of pods, so vegetable seedlings are planted between the cacao trees for short-term income. The plan is to eventually start making and selling chocolate too.

What does this project have to do with watershed connections? The 70,000 cacao trees planted over 173 acres (70 hectares) of land are preventing deforestation—farmers with no crops to sell often cut down and sell trees instead. And thanks to the roots of the cacao trees anchoring the soil and holding on to water in the soil, two of the community's streams now have good flow and don't dry up.

SPROUTING ROOFS

Like all cities, Ecuador's capital city, Quito, is awash with paved streets, buildings and cars. It's a sprawling place of impervious surfaces, blanketed by poor air quality.

A young plant biologist, Liliana Jaramillo Pazmiño, is changing that with green roofs. She is figuring out which native Ecuadorian plants grow especially well on roofs. Liliana wants to transform Quito into a city of high-up green spaces with plants to absorb pollutants from the air and soak up rainwater to reduce flooding.

Growing plants on rooftops reduces pollution and rainwater runoff in cities.
GEOGIF/GETTY IMAGES

CONNECTIONS THAT COUNT

Walking along waterways to raise awareness, helping the next generation reconnect with their land, reviving villages and ecosystems with ancient practices, and planting seeds in fields and on roofs. These stories show that small actions make a big difference. It's the connections that count.

You can connect with your watershed and your community to make a difference in many ways. I bet you're already doing some of the things listed below, and that's awesome! Choose a few more of them and challenge yourself, your friends and your family to help watersheds near and far.

Learn your address

Find out the name of the watershed where you live. Haul out an old-fashioned paper map or bring up Google Maps on a computer. Once you've found your nearest river, figure out which way is downstream. If you can visit the river, great. If not, do some more googling or head to a library for more information.

Explore your watershed

Learn about the features of your local waterways. Are they surrounded by natural land cover or by human land uses? Do they face pressures such as being confined in concrete channels, or stripped of their natural vegetation, or trampled by livestock, or filled with garbage? Talk with family, friends and teachers about your watershed's features and pressures.

Join a local watershed group

Many communities have active groups of volunteers who look after their local waterways. They remove trash, plant riparian vegetation, test water quality and talk with the public at community events. Google terms like *stream keepers, lake keepers* and *river guardians* to find a group near you.

Calculate your ecological footprint

Figure out how many resources—water, energy, food, transportation—you use every day. This gives you a starting point for deciding what you can change. Then commit to making changes, such as using less water and electricity, eating fewer animal products, walking or using public transit more.

Buy less, use less...of everything

Every item we buy has a water footprint. Water gets used to grow, make and transport everything: the apple in your lunch, your clothes, your chair. Water also gets used in your daily actions: drinking a glass of water, brushing your teeth, turning on a light. The less stuff we buy and use, the less water we use, and the more water is available for a watershed nearby.

Dispose of used items carefully

Sinks and toilets are not garbage bins! Toss items like used dental floss, Band-Aids and wipes in the garbage. Keep fruit and veggie stickers away from the kitchen sink. If your family has expired medicine or old paint or motor oil, ask your parents not to dump them down the drain. Instead take them to a pharmacy or a recycling facility for proper disposal.

Plant a tree, or two or three

Tree roots hold the soil and allow rainwater to soak into the ground. If you have a yard, plant trees, bushes and grasses that are native to your region. If you don't have a yard, look for a community tree-planting program. Get your hands dirty for your watershed's health!

Get connected

Participate in events like World Rivers Day. Talk with your family, friends and teachers about watershed connections and health. Share your ideas for making changes in your own lifestyle. Challenge others to join you!

Be watershed wise

Healthy communities and healthy people need healthy watersheds. As you've read in this book, the connections run deep. Animals, plants, people, water, land...everything and everyone connects to the others. Through our connections we can do good things and not-so-good things. Let's do more of the first and less of the second. Let's all help watersheds, so that watersheds can help us in return.

Resources

Print

Dobson, Clive, and Gregor Gilpin Beck. *Watersheds: A Practical Handbook for Healthy Water.* Buffalo, NY: Firefly Books, 1999.

Jones, Kari. *Ours to Share: Coexisting in a Crowded World.* Victoria, BC: Orca Book Publishers, 2019.

Mulder, Michelle. *Every Last Drop: Bringing Clean Water Home.* Victoria, BC: Orca Book Publishers, 2014.

Peters, Marilee. *10 Rivers that Shaped the World.* Toronto, ON: Annick Press, 2015.

Rae, Rowena. *Chemical World: Science in Our Daily Lives.* Victoria, BC: Orca Book Publishers, 2020.

Robertson, Joanne. *The Water Walker.* Toronto, ON: Second Story Press, 2017.

Online

Global Footprint Network, What Is Your Ecological Footprint?: footprintcalculator.org

International Rivers: internationalrivers.org

National Aeronautics and Space Administration (NASA), Earth Observatory, World of Change (time-lapse photos): earthobservatory.nasa.gov/world-of-change

National Geographic, Resource Library, Watershed: nationalgeographic.org/topics/resource-library-watershed

United Nations (UN) Environment Program, Young Champions of the Earth: unenvironment.org/youngchampions

US Geological Survey (USGS), Watersheds and Drainage Basins: usgs.gov/special-topic/water-science-school/science/watersheds-and-drainage-basins

Water Footprint Calculator: watercalculator.org

World Rivers Day: worldriversday.com

Apps

WWF Free Rivers: An app for exploring rivers and their surrounding watersheds

Glossary

anthropogenic—relating to human activity

aqueduct—a series of pipes, tunnels, canals and bridges to carry water for long distances

aquifer—an underground bed of rocks, sand and/or gravel that has water (groundwater) within it

biodiversity hotspot—a place where an exceptionally wide array of animal and plant species lives

catchment basin—the entire land area, or "basin," that catches precipitation and drains it into a particular body of water; also called a watershed

civilization—a complex human society with cultural practices and technologies

dam—a barrier built across a river channel to control (hold back or release) water

daylighting—uncovering a buried stream to open it up to daylight

deciduous—having leaves that shed every year

deforestation—removing trees from the land

delta—the triangular or fan-shaped area of islands and channels at the mouth of a river

dike—a bank or wall built along the edge of a river channel to control where the water flows

ecological footprint—the amount of environmental resources (land, water, energy, materials) it takes to support a particular lifestyle

ecosystem—all the plants and animals plus all the nonliving things (rocks, soil, water) that exist together in a particular place

ecosystem services—the things nature provides "free of charge" that sustain human life and survival

erodes—wears down or slowly destroys something

estuary—the place where river water mixes with tidal ocean water

evaporate—turn from a liquid into vapor (gas)

fertile—rich in nutrients and capable of growing large quantities of crops

floodplain—the land on either side of a river that floods during times of high water flow

freshet—the flooding of a stream or river due to heavy rain or quickly melting snow

glacier—a slow-moving river of ice made from compacted snow in mountain and polar regions

groundwater—water in the ground (see *aquifer*)

headwaters—the high point of land where a river starts

hydrologic cycle—the continuous movement of water between the oceans, atmosphere and land; the cycle

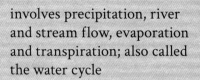

involves precipitation, river and stream flow, evaporation and transpiration; also called the water cycle

impervious—not allowing water or other fluids to get through

Industrial Revolution—a period in history that started in the mid-1700s in Britain with the invention of steam engines, and changed society from an agricultural to a manufacturing economy

irrigation—the watering of land to encourage crops or other plants to grow

land cover—the things that are on the surface of the land, such as grasses, trees, rocks, sand, bare soil and water

land use—what humans do on or to the land, such as building, paving surfaces, farming, mining, harvesting trees and laying pipelines

meanders—(noun) the wide bends in a river

mouth—the part of a stream or river where it flows into a larger body of water (river, lake, ocean)

outflow—the part of a stream or river where it flows into a larger body of water (river, lake, ocean); also the part of a lake where a stream or river flows out of it

precipitation—water that falls from the atmosphere as rain, snow or hail

reservoir—an artificial lake, usually made by building a dam across a river to hold back water

riparian zone—the land alongside rivers and streams

salinization—the process by which salts build up in the soil, eventually making it toxic to many plants

saturated—full of moisture

sedimentary—formed by the accumulation of layers of sediments that solidify

source—the start of a river at a high point of land

transpiration—the process of water being released from plants through their leaves, stems and other parts

tributary—a stream that flows into a larger stream or a lake

water cycle—the continuous movement of water between the oceans, atmosphere and land; the cycle involves precipitation, river and stream flow, evaporation and transpiration; also called the hydrologic cycle

water table—the top of the zone in the ground where all the cracks and pores in the rocks are saturated with water (the saturation zone)

watershed—the entire land area, or "basin," that catches precipitation and drains it into a particular body of water; also called a catchment basin

weir—a type of dam built across a river channel to control water flow or divert water elsewhere

wetlands—an area of land saturated with water; examples include marshes, bogs, fens and swamps

Index

Page numbers in **bold** indicate an image caption.

activism: make a difference, 42; tree planting, **31**, 32, 40–41, 42

agriculture. *See* farmland

Amazon River watershed, 23

Angkor, **11**

Angola, 39

Antarctica, 23

aqueducts, 13, 28, 44

aquifers (groundwater), 15, 20–21, 27, 40, 44

Aral Sea, 29–30

Australia, 12, 28

Austria, **25**

Britannia Creek dam, **27**

British Columbia, watershed, 8, 22

cacao trees, 40–41

Cambodia, **11**, **14**

canals, 12, 14–15

canyons, 18, **22**, 23

catchment basins, 8, 44. *See also* watersheds

Chile, watershed, **18**

China, **34**; canals, 14–15

cities: confined rivers, 35–37; flooding in, 34, 35–37; green roofs, 41; growth of, **34**, 37; reservoirs, 13, 34; riverbank uses, **21**, **33**, 37

civilizations, 11, 12, 44

climate change, 18, 22

coal mining, 15–16

Colorado River: canyons, **22**, 23; Hoover Dam, 24

community, 6–7, 42

Congo River, 34

Costa, Adjany, 39

Cyprus, 11

dams, 24–28, 44; and irrigation, 11, 12, 28

da Vinci, Leonardo, 15

daylighting, 37, 44

Day of Action for Rivers, **26**

deforestation, 15, 30–32, 44

deltas, 10–11, 19, 44

dikes, 14–15, 44

drinking water. *See* fresh water

Ducks Unlimited, 40

earthquakes, 23

ecological footprint, 17, 44; calculation of, 42

ecosystems: biodiversity, 39; defined, 9, 44; estuaries, 19, 27, 44; habitat loss, 26, 28, 32; wetlands, 20

ecosystem services, 30, 34, 44

Ecuador, 41

Egypt, Nile River delta, 10–11

Elwha River, dam removal, **25**, 27

estuaries, 19, 27, 44

farmland: history, 10–15; riverbank uses, **30**; and salinization, 12; tree planting, 40–41. *See also* irrigation

fish: habitat loss, 19, 30, 31; salmon spawning, 26, 27

floodplains, 23, 26, 44; loss of, 35

floodwaters: control of, 20, 26, 35–36; and impervious surfaces, 22, 31, 33, 45; seasonal cycles, 22–23

forests: role of, 30–32; transpiration, 21, 22; tree planting, **31**, 32, 40–41, 42

fossil fuels, 16–17

Fraser River watershed, 8, 22

freshet, 22, 44

fresh water: conservation, 38, 40, 42; contamination, **10**; respect for, 38; supply systems, 12

Ganges River, 36; delta, **19**

glaciers, 18, 22, 44

Global Footprint Network, 17, 43

Grand Canal (China), 14

Grand Canyon, 23

Great Lakes, 19, 38

groundwater (aquifer), 15, 20–21, 44; depletion, 27, 40

Hanging Glacier, **18**

headwaters, 8, 18, 44

Hoover Dam, **24**

Houston, **33**

human impact: of ancient civilizations, 10–15; on aquifers, 20, 27, 33, 34; deforestation, 15; early humans, 9–10; and the Industrial Revolution, 15–17; land use, 21; and manufacturing, **16**, 38

hydroelectricity, 24–25

hydrologic cycle (water cycle), 22, 44–45

impervious surfaces, 22, 31, 33, 45

India, 10, 35–36, 39–40

Indigenous Peoples, 26–27, 38

Industrial Revolution, 15–17, 45

International Rivers, 24–25, 43

irrigation: canals, 12, 14–15; dams, 11, 12, 24–25, 28; and salinization, 29–30; systems, 10–11, 14–15, 45

Istanbul, Roman aqueduct, **13**

johads, 40

Kazakhstan, 29–30

Kvirila River, **21**

lakes: city reservoirs, **11**, 13, 34; dam reservoirs, 24, **25**; formation, 19; salinization of, 29–30

Lake St. Clair, 19

Lake Superior, 19

Index  (continued)

Lake Vanda, 23
land cover, 21, 45
land use, 21, 45
Los Angeles River, **35**

Mabulo, Louise, 40–**41**
Mandamin, Josephine, 38
Marble Canyon, **22**
meanders, 18, **19**, 35, 45
Mediterranean Sea, 10–11
Mexico City, 27
Minjiang River, canals, 14–15
Mississippi River, **19**; watershed, **9**
Missouri River, meander, **19**
monsoon rains, **11**, 23, 35–36, 40
Mount St. Helens, 28
Myanmar, **26**

natural resources, 16–17, 31
New York City, 34
Nile River delta, 10–11
North American Great Lakes, 19, 38

oceans: and climate change, 22;
    estuaries, 19, 44
Ogallala Aquifer, 20
Okavango River wetlands, 39
outflow, 19, 45

Pazmiño, Liliana Jaramillo, 41
Peltier, Autumn, 38
Philippines, 40–41
pollution: human impact, 16–17, 42;
    and stormwater, 22, 34; water
    filtration, 20
precipitation, 8, 22, 40, 45; and
    flooding, 23, 35–36; storage, **11**, 40
public awareness: activists, 38–41;
    of local waterways, 6–7; make a
    difference, 42; watering of lawns, 40;
    World Rivers Day, 39, 43

Rae, Rowena, 6–7, 23, 28
rainwater: and flooding, 23, 35–36;
    precipitation, 8, 22, 45; storage, **11**, 40
Ramsar Wetlands of International
    Importance, 33–34
reservoirs: and cities, **11**, 13, 34; of
    dams, **25**, 26; defined, 45
resources, 43
Rio River watershed, **18**
riparian zone, 19, 26, 45
riverbank uses, **21**, **30**, **33**, 37
rivers: confined, 35–37; flooding, 20,
    35–36; impact of dams, 26; impact
    of sediments, 19, 28, 31; as power
    source, 15, 24–25; systems, 8, 18–19
roadways, 22, 31, 33
Roman aqueducts, 13

salinization, 12, 29–30, 45
salmon, habitat, 26, 27
Savery, Thomas, 16
sediments, 19, 28, 31
Seoul, 37
Shanghai, **34**
Singh, Rajendra, 39–40
Snowy River, 28
soil: erosion, 31; rainwater absorption,
    39–40; in river deltas, 19;
    salinization, 12, 30
South Korea, 37
standing water, 19
steam power, 15–16
stormwater, 34, 35–36, 37
Sumerian people, 12
Summerland, BC, 40

technology, 12–16, 24–25
Tigris and Euphrates Rivers, 11, 12
transpiration, 22, 45
tree planting, **31**, 32, 40–41, 42
tributary, 14, 45

United States: Ogallala Aquifer, 20–21;
    roadways, 33; watershed map, **9**
urban design. *See* cities
Uzbekistan, 29–30

Vancouver, BC, 8, 37
volcanic eruptions, 23, 28

water cycle, 21–22, 45
water footprint, 38, 40, 42
Water Footprint Calculator, 43
watersheds: defined, 8–9, 45; health
    of, 6–7, 37; human impact, 16–17;
    protection of, 39; seasonal cycles,
    22–23; structure of, 18–21
water table, 20–21, 45
waterwheels, 13, 15
Watt, James, 16
weirs, 11, 45
wells, 11, 20, 40
wetlands: cranes, **20**; defined, 20, 45;
    loss of, 32, 35; protection of, 33–34,
    39, 40; water filtration, 34
wildlife, 19, 20, 39
World Rivers Day, 39, 43

Acknowledgments

Many people helped me as I researched and wrote this book. Thank you to Sarah Harvey, who acquired the project for Orca Book Publishers, and to Kirstie Hudson, my editor at Orca, who edited my writing with attention and care and also asked excellent questions that helped me improve the book.

I'm very grateful to the following people who reviewed and commented on the manuscript: Mark Angelo, river conservationist and founder of World Rivers Day, Vancouver, BC; Ken Ashley, chair of the BC Institute of Technology's Rivers Institute, Vancouver; Steven Mithen, professor of archaeology at University of Reading, Berkshire, UK; and Ellen Wohl, professor of geosciences at Colorado State University, Fort Collins.

Thank you to Louise Mabulo, chef and founder of the Cacao Project in San Fernando, Philippines, for information about her work and for allowing me to include some of her photos.

I also thank Alyson Skinner and Mark Angelo for additional photos.

My writing friend and critique partner, Carolyn Combs, has encouraged me through all my writing (both successes and failures). Thank you, Carolyn!

Exploring and learning about watersheds has been a large part of my life from childhood, through university and to the present day. For sharing in these explorations with me over the years, I thank my parents, Ann Skidmore and Angus Rae; my sister, Elspeth Rae; my friends and mentors from the University of Ottawa and Laval University, especially Andrew Wilson; my hiking friend, Sharilynn Wardrop; my partner, Travis Commandeur; and, most especially, my children, Genevieve and Madeleine, who not only explore nature with me but also are unfailingly cheerful about my writing, even when it interferes with family life.

BRADY JENKINS

ROWENA RAE worked as a biologist in Canada and New Zealand before becoming a freelance writer and editor and a children's author. She is the author of *Chemical World: Science in Our Daily Lives*, which is part of the Orca Footprints series. She writes both fiction and nonfiction from her home in Victoria, British Columbia, which she shares with her two book-loving children.